DATE DUE

D1402762

Just the Facts

# Body Piercing and Tattoos

Paul Mason

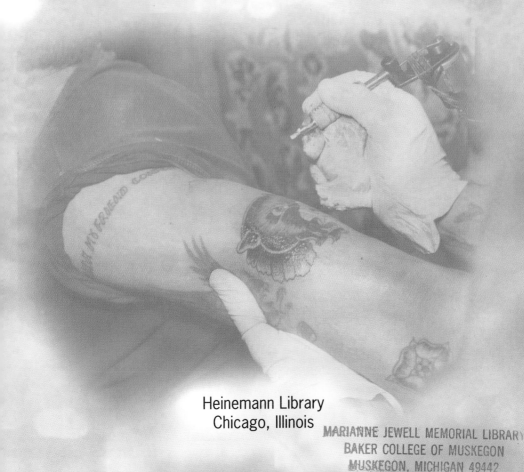

Heinemann Library
Chicago, Illinois

Customer Service  888-454-2279
Visit our website at www.heinemannlibrary.com

Designed by Jane Hawkins
Originated by Ambassador Litho Ltd.
Printed and bound in China by South China Printing Company

07 06 05 04 03
10 9 8 7 6 5 4 3 2 1

**Library of Congress Cataloging-in-Publication Data**
Mason, Paul, 1967-
   Body piercing and tattoos / Paul Mason.
      p. cm. -- (Just the facts)
Summary: Describes the history of body piercing and tattooing, as well
as what motivates people to get a piercing or a tattoo, how to care for
them, problems that can arise, and legal issues surrounding them.
Includes bibliographical references and index.
   ISBN 1-4034-0817-3 (lib. bdg.)
   1. Tattooing--Juvenile literature. 2.  Body piercing--Juvenile
literature. [1. Tattooing. 2. Body piercing.]  I. Title. II. Series.
   GT2345 .M36 2003
   391.65--dc21

                              2002010936

**Acknowledgments**
The author and publisher are grateful to the following for permission to reproduce copyright material:
Cover photograph: Peter M. Fisher/Corbis Stock Market (bottom).
p. 4 Suzanne Murphy/Rex Features; p. 5 Tim Mosenfelder/Corbis; p. 6 John Walmsley Photography; pp. 7, 17 Richard Young/Rex Features; p. 8 Archivo Iconografico, S.A./Corbis; pp. 9, 36 Norman Rockwell/AKG; p. 10 C. M. Dixon; pp. 12, 43 Reinhard Kreuse/Reuters/Popperfoto; p. 13 Horace Bristol/Corbis; p. 14 Bettman/Corbis; p. 19, 50–51 Tony Savino/Rex Features; pp. 20, 21, 45 Nils Jorgensen/Rex Features; pp. 22–23 Cesare Bonazza/Rex Features; p. 24 Topham Picturepoint; p. 25 Brian Bohannon/Associated Press; pp. 26–27 Malcolm Earl/Medipics; p. 29 Tony Gutierrez/Associated Press; p. 31 Sipa/Rex Features; p. 32 Dr. P. Marazzi/Science Photo Library; p. 33 Eva Magazine/Rex Features; pp. 34, 35 Medipics; p. 37 Douglas Pizac/Associated Press; p. 38 Tim Coleman/Rex Features; p. 41 Chat Magazine/Rex Features; p. 42 Peter M. Fisher/Corbis; p. 44 Mike Alsford/Rex Features; p. 47 John Reynolds/Popperfoto; pp. 48–49 Hank Morgan/Science Photo Library.

Our special thanks to Pamela G. Richards, M.Ed., for her help in the preparation of the book.

Some words appear in bold, **like this.** You can find out what they mean by looking in the glossary.

# Contents

# Piercing and Tattooing

Body piercing and tattooing have probably never been as popular as they are today. Tattoos especially seem to be everywhere. Piercings, which are often hidden under clothing, can be harder to spot. But you only have to walk down a busy street in New York City, Chicago, or Los Angeles to see a variety of people with nose studs, navel rings, and pierced eyebrows and tongues.

Less than 50 years ago in the United States, body piercing and tattooing were not common. Teens in the 1950s and early 1960s, for example, would have found it much more difficult to get piercings and tattoos than they do today. For one thing, there were far fewer tattoo parlors and piercing studios. For another, people had a very different view of piercings and tattoos. One woman who was a teenager in the 1960s remembered: "I desperately wanted to have my ears pierced. It seems like nothing today, but at the time it was a very big deal. My mother told me—very clearly and many times—that having your ears pierced was 'low-class.' She made it pretty clear that if I came home with pierced ears I might as well pack my bags and leave, as I'd have brought shame on the whole family."

Pierced noses, eyebrows, navels, and other body parts were so unusual that most people would have been amazed to hear about them. Tattoos were more common than piercings after World

**This woman wears a piercing in her nose as part of her traditional dress.**

War II, but were mainly associated with men serving in the Army or Navy.

In the recent past—even twenty years ago—piercings and tattoos were seen as a way of rebelling against polite society, so it is easy to think that they have always been seen like that. This is not the case. From **Polynesian** chiefs to the cream of high society, from the rain forests of South America to the household of Queen Victoria, body piercing and tattooing have a long and varied history.

**ff One must *be* a work of art, or *wear* a work of art. JJ**

(Oscar Wilde)

**Mary J. Blige is one of many musicians who sport tattoos.**

# What Are Piercing and Tattooing?

## Body piercing

Body piercing involves pushing a sharp object through a person's skin, so that it goes under the outer layer and comes back out through the skin in a different place. Various objects, usually metal jewelry, can then be put into the hole to keep it open. After a while, the flesh around the hole heals naturally and the jewelry can then be changed.

Soft flesh, such as an earlobe, is most suitable for piercing, but almost any part of the body can be pierced. Noses, eyebrows, cheeks, nipples, navels, lips, tongues—all these and more are pierced by fans of body piercing. Why people choose to have their body pierced is much harder to explain than how it is done.

Many people have piercings done as a kind of body decoration. Eyebrow rings among U.S. teens, for example, are purely decorative. In some cultures, a piercing may have a special significance, such as showing that a boy has reached maturity and become a man.

# Tattooing

Tattooing is the practice of making a visible design under someone's skin. Tattoos are made by putting ink through the outer layer of skin and into the layer beneath. This second layer, known as the **dermis,** moves very little during a person's lifetime and does not break down, so tattoos are **permanent.** Most people's tattoos have special significance to them, making each tattoo personal to the individual.

There are various ways of getting tattoo ink into the flesh, but all involve piercing or cutting the skin. This is usually done using an electric-powered device that pushes a needle up and down, piercing the skin on each downstroke and injecting a small amount of ink into the flesh.

Other, less permanent, tattoo-like skin markings are also sometimes used. These include **henna** tattoos and transfers that are applied to the skin and eventually rub off.

**Singer Mel C. from the group Spice Girls has a tattoo in Chinese characters that means "girl power" or, literally, "woman" and "strength." Her mother has the same tattoo.**

# History of Body Piercing

Piercing has been practiced throughout the world for many centuries. People in the past were sometimes pierced. Cleopatra, for example, is said to have had piercings. A 4,000-year-old clay figurine from Iran was found with multiple-pierced ears. Gold earrings have been found on the island of Cyprus from 2,200 years ago, showing that people living there had their ears pierced.

## Coming of age

Other piercings have been done as a way of marking a significant event in someone's life, such as the moment when a boy became a man or when a woman got married. In Central Africa, ancient tribal customs suggested that a woman would be more valuable as a wife if she had a particular piercing. Girls who were about to become women attended a special ceremony at which the piercing was performed. The ceremony included a **symbolic** sacrifice of their girlhood.

**This ancient Egyptian bust shows that people were wearing earrings at least 4,000 years ago.**

## Stretched earlobes

Throughout Asia, there are examples of people having pierced ears. These people wore heavy earrings to stretch their earlobes. A stone head, found in China, from around 550 C.E. depicts a person with pierced ears and stretched lobes, as does a Chinese mural from around 1400 C.E. This practice is still common in parts of Asia today, such as Borneo.

## Portable currency

One type of piercing was done as a way of storing wealth. In the days of sailing ships, sailors needed to store their money in a way that was both easily available and useable wherever their ship traveled. So they had their ears pierced and inserted a gold ring into the piercing. Gold could then be shaved off or added to the ring as needed, and gold could buy goods in whichever port the ships docked.

## Social status

The Tlingit of Alaska wore nose rings as a mark of distinction and prestige. Both men and women had nose rings. Nose piercing was also popular in ancient India and Mexico. Today, women in India and Pakistan, along with many other people around the world, continue to wear nose rings. The position of a nose ring can mean different things to different people.

**Some Roman gladiators were known to have had piercings.**

# History of Tattoos

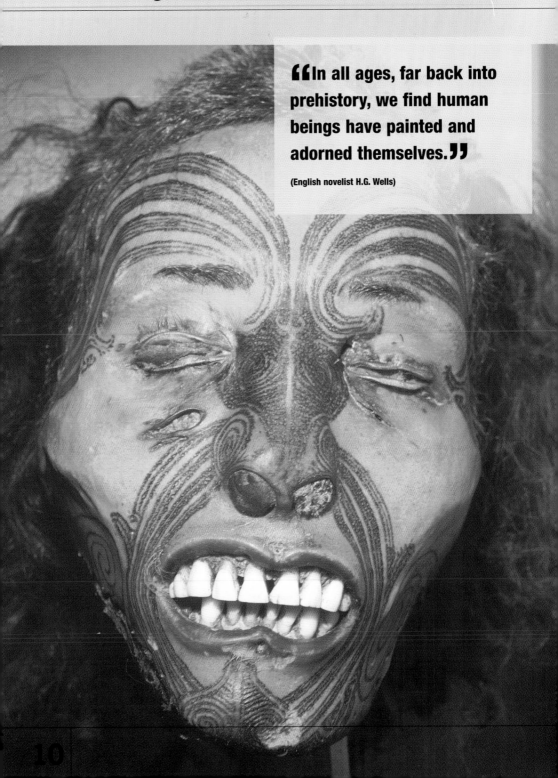

**"In all ages, far back into prehistory, we find human beings have painted and adorned themselves."**

(English novelist H.G. Wells)

No one knows for certain when the first tattoo was done. Skin usually decays after death, so it is very difficult to know when tattoos were first made. Evidence of ancient tattoos has come mainly from places where bodies have been **mummified,** preserving their skin and leaving behind the design that the mummified person wore in life.

## Preserved skin

In 1993, an ancient mummified body was discovered in a high, windswept area of Siberia, in Russia, known as the Pastures of Heaven. The mummy was of a woman, who became known as the Ice Maiden. In life she had been a priestess. Probably because of this, her skin was covered in bright blue tattoos of animal figures, representing the creatures her people would have relied on for food. The Ice Maiden had been frozen in the Siberian ice for more than 2,400 years, making her one of the oldest known tattooed women. There is evidence that ancient Egyptians had tattoos even earlier than the Ice Maiden, in about 2000 B.C.E.

Left: The mummified head of this **Maori** chief shows the face tattoos he wore in life.

In 1992, a mummified, tattooed man's body was found in the European Alps, on the border between Italy and Austria. The Ice Man, as he became known, had been buried in a **glacier** for roughly 4,000 years, making his tattoos as old as the ancient Egyptian ones.

## Tattooed warriors

In about 100 C.E., invading Roman armies reached northern Britain. There they encountered Pict warriors who lived in the area that is now Scotland. The Pict fighters were covered in blue tattoos. The name Pict is believed to be from the Latin word *picti*, meaning "the painted men." The Pict were so fierce that the **Roman legions** could not subdue them. Instead, the Romans were forced to build Hadrian's Wall along the northern border of England to keep out their tattooed enemies.

The purposes of these ancient tattoos are not certain. They may have been purely for decoration, but are more likely to have been a sign of a person's rank or position. Having a tattoo today can be painful, but it may have been more so then. Tattooing would have been a dangerous process because of the risk of a cut becoming infected.

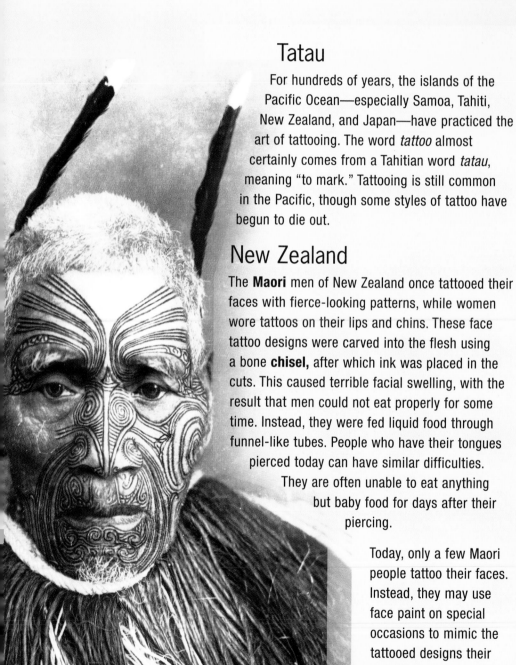

## Tatau

For hundreds of years, the islands of the Pacific Ocean—especially Samoa, Tahiti, New Zealand, and Japan—have practiced the art of tattooing. The word *tattoo* almost certainly comes from a Tahitian word *tatau*, meaning "to mark." Tattooing is still common in the Pacific, though some styles of tattoo have begun to die out.

## New Zealand

The **Maori** men of New Zealand once tattooed their faces with fierce-looking patterns, while women wore tattoos on their lips and chins. These face tattoo designs were carved into the flesh using a bone **chisel,** after which ink was placed in the cuts. This caused terrible facial swelling, with the result that men could not eat properly for some time. Instead, they were fed liquid food through funnel-like tubes. People who have their tongues pierced today can have similar difficulties. They are often unable to eat anything but baby food for days after their piercing.

Today, only a few Maori people tattoo their faces. Instead, they may use face paint on special occasions to mimic the tattooed designs their ancestors wore.

## Samoa

On the Samoan islands, tattooing was a mark of a man's ability to bear pain. A man without tattoos in Samoan society would have been thought of as a weakling.

Samoan tattoos were applied using a special comb. The teeth of the comb were dipped in ink then tapped into the skin, puncturing it and leaving the ink in the flesh beneath. A complicated design could take as long as six months to finish and was applied in a specially-built tattooing hut.

## Japan

Japanese tattoos are famous, incorporating many different colors to create some of the most intricate designs in the world. Traditionally, people who had full-body tattoos in Japan belonged almost entirely to an organized group of criminals called *yakuza*. Even a simple Japanese carp tattoo on a person's shoulder took months to finish, and full-body tattoos took years to complete.

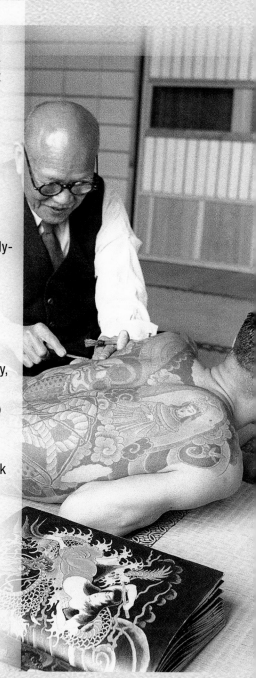

**Many *yakuza*, an organized crime group in Japan, had tattoos that covered their entire bodies, ending only at the neck, wrists, and ankles.**

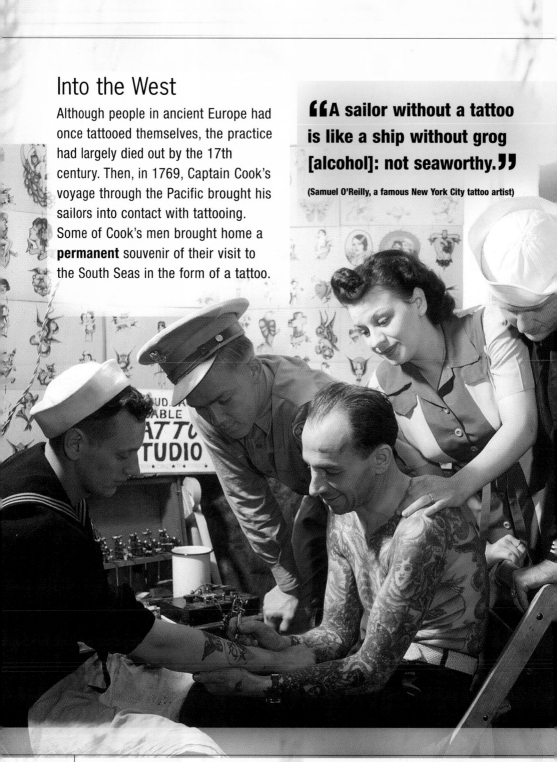

## Into the West

Although people in ancient Europe had once tattooed themselves, the practice had largely died out by the 17th century. Then, in 1769, Captain Cook's voyage through the Pacific brought his sailors into contact with tattooing. Some of Cook's men brought home a **permanent** souvenir of their visit to the South Seas in the form of a tattoo.

**"A sailor without a tattoo is like a ship without grog [alcohol]: not seaworthy."**

(Samuel O'Reilly, a famous New York City tattoo artist)

At the time, sailors were just about the toughest, most unruly people around. Ever since Cook's explorations, tattoos have been associated with sailors. This is perhaps the reason tattoos gained a bad reputation.

People in North America and Europe became fascinated by tattoos. During the 18th and 19th centuries, tattooed Indians or Pacific Islanders drew great crowds of people who were willing to pay to see their unusual skin markings. It was not long before an increasing number of tattooists set up shop and offered to give people tattoos. Their best customers were sailors and soldiers. Far fewer people from outside the armed forces wanted to have tattoos.

During the 19th and 20th centuries, many people had a bad impression of tattoos. Many thought they were a sign that someone was rebellious and **antisocial.**

**Left: Yet another tattoo is added to a sailor's already colorful skin in a New York tattoo studio.**

The U.S. government even tried to limit tattoos among the armed forces. The 1909 recruitment regulations stated: "indecent or obscene tattooing is cause for rejection." This regulation caused a mini-boom in the tattooing industry in the 1940s, as young men flocked to cover up their rude tattoos so that they could enlist to fight in World War II.

### The Great Omi

Perhaps the strangest tattooed person ever was a carnival star named "The Great Omi." Omi—whose real name, Horace Ridler, was known to very few people during his lifetime—had been an officer in the British Army and came from a respectable, middle-class background. A series of financial disasters left him almost penniless, and he decided to turn himself into a **freak-show** star. Starting in 1927, the Great Omi was tattooed all over to look like a zebra. The tattoos on Omi's face and head alone required fifteen million needle pricks, and the entire process took more than a year. His tattooist noted dryly, and with massive understatement, that the tattooing "must have caused some pain and distress."

# Motivations

Today there is usually more than one reason behind a person's decision to have a tattoo or piercing.

## Rebellion

Years ago, almost the only people who had tattoos were the tough and unruly: sailors, soldiers, **Hell's Angels,** and criminals. Having a tattoo marked a person as an outsider, someone who did not play by the rules. Tattoos and piercings are still unusual enough for people who have them to be seen as rebels. People who are heavily tattooed or pierced look different. They have rebelled against the usual rules about how a person should look.

## Rites of passage

A rite of passage is a ceremony or event that marks a change or turning point in someone's life, such as becoming an adult or getting married. Actress Pamela Anderson once said that "tattoos are **symbolic** of the most important moments of your life." Of course, as time goes by, tattoos and piercings can take on a different meaning. Pamela realized this herself, when she imagined the day when: "my sons' first girlfriends come over and I'm all wrinkled up in a chair with tattoos all sagging down to my ankles."

## Aspirations

Some people use tattoos as a way of displaying their goals. Several athletes, for example, have had **Olympic rings** tattooed on their bodies to show how much they wanted to compete in the Olympic Games.

## Love

Some people have the names of their loved ones tattooed on their skin. This is not without risk: "Mom" and "Dad" are pretty safe, but other loved ones can change. Almost all professional tattooists can tell stories about people asking to have the name of a former boyfriend or girlfriend covered up with a new design.

> **"I go all the time now—once every four months. It's very addictive."**
>
> **(U.S. comedian Roseanne)**

## Sadness

Sometimes a tattoo or piercing is done to remember a sad event, such as the death of a friend. Actress Alyssa Milano once said, "I've always gotten them [tattoos] at times when I was sad about something […] relationship problems or the fact that it had rained every day for a month."

## No significance!

People do not always have a reason for getting a tattoo or piercing. Sometimes the only reason is that it looked good or felt right. Many say that once they had one tattoo or piercing, they wanted to have more.

**Actress Angelina Jolie had actor Billy Bob Thornton's name tattooed on her arm soon after she married him. By the summer of 2002, the two had split up.**

# How Tattooing Works

Tattooing involves placing ink under the outer layer of skin, into the **dermis.** The cells of the dermis are very stable, so ink that is added to them stays almost exactly where it is for as long as the skin is alive.

Around the world, various tools have been used for tattooing, including needles, knives, **chisels,** and a needle and thread. In 1891, Samuel O'Reilly transformed the art of tattooing with his new, electric-powered invention— the first automatic tattoo machine. Based on Thomas Edison's electric pen, O'Reilly's device had a needle that moved up and down like a mini-jackhammer, carrying ink into the skin with each downward stroke. Modern tattoo machines work in a similar way.

## High-speed tattoos

Today's electric tattoo machines puncture the skin between 50 and 3,000 times a minute. They use a **sterilized** needle that drives tiny particles of ink about 1/8 inch (3 millimeters) deep into the dermis before withdrawing to collect more ink. The ink travels to the needle through tubes. The machine is controlled using a foot pedal like the one on an ordinary sewing machine.

Almost all tattoos are done following a **stencil** or outline of the design. This is stuck to the skin and allows the customer to say whether they want it bigger, smaller, or in a different place. Some customers decide at this point that they do not want the tattoo done at all. One problem with homemade tattoos is that they are often done without a stencil, so the tattoo ends up looking poorly drawn or in the wrong position.

Once the customer is happy with the size and position of the stencil, the actual tattoo is begun. First, the skin is cleaned and prepared with antiseptic soap and water. Then, the tattooist makes an outline of the design using a single needle, usually with black ink. Next, the outline is thickened and the shading is added, still usually in black ink. The area is cleaned again, and then color is added. After being wiped clean a final time, the tattoo is complete.

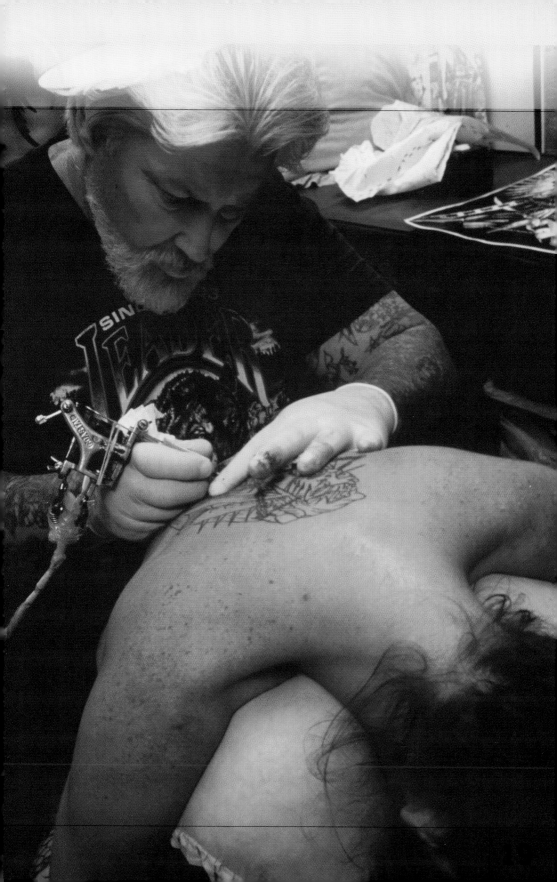

# How Piercing Is Done

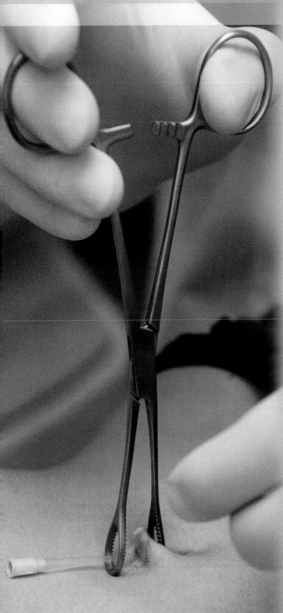

Clamps are used to hold the skin in the correct position for piercing.

Piercing punctures the skin more deeply than tattooing and is potentially more painful, although piercing is a far quicker process. Some piercings are like minor **surgery,** and occasionally an ethyl chloride spray is used to numb the area before the piercing is done. Most piercings are performed without the use of any kind of painkiller.

The area to be pierced is pinched together with clamps. Then a hollow needle in a plastic tube coated in **lubricant** is pushed through the skin and flesh by the piercer, hollowing out a passage. The needle is pulled out, leaving the plastic tube in the passage. Jewelry is then pushed into the tube. The tube is eased out of the **wound,** leaving only the jewelry behind.

In some places, such as beauty salons, piercings are done using an instrument called a **piercing gun.** This is a mechanical device loaded with a stud. It is used both to make the piercing and as the jewelry that keeps the passage open. The flesh to be pierced is placed inside the top of the gun, then the stud is lined up with the desired spot. The handle is pulled to release the stud and force it through the skin. On the exit side of the wound, a fastener is added to the stud to keep it in place. Professional piercers usually refuse to use piercing guns because they are potentially less **hygienic** than single-use hollow needles and can squash the area around the piercing site.

The jewelry used for piercing is usually made of highly polished surgical steel that contains nickel. If the person being pierced has an **allergy** to nickel, jewelry made of titanium or 18-carat gold is used instead. Each of these helps prevent the wound from becoming infected.

After the piercing is finished, the wound is cleaned and, if necessary, bandaged. Bandaging is normally used on a piercing where the surrounding flesh may move around a lot and cause further bleeding (such as a navel piercing). Many piercing studios will also give their customers written advice on how to care for their piercing.

**A customer is shown her new piercing in a mirror.**

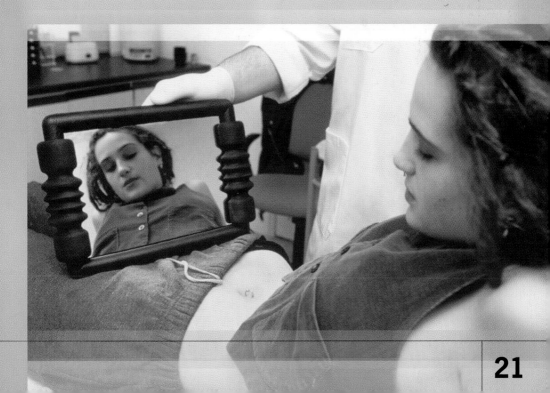

# Cosmetic Tattooing

A cosmetic tattoo is one that is done for reasons of personal appearance, almost like wearing makeup or having a haircut. People often get cosmetic tattoos for use as **permanent** makeup or to hide a disfigurement or defect of some sort.

The earliest modern cosmetic tattooing was done in Britain roughly 100 years ago. In the early 1900s, it became fashionable for upper-class women in London to have healthy-looking flushed cheeks. One way for them to achieve this look was to wear makeup, but at the time makeup was thought of as unsuitable for upper-class women. Instead, some of the most fashionable and richest women in the country came to beauty salons to have color tattooed on their cheeks. As one tattooist remembered in his memoirs: "The word 'tattooing' was never mentioned." Instead, these fashionable women came to the beauty salon to have a "permanent beauty treatment."

**A cosmetic tattooist carefully applies color to a woman's lips.**

## War veterans

Following World War I and II, skilled tattooists worked alongside doctors to help men who had suffered injuries during the fighting. Often, the men's faces had been affected by heat or **shrapnel,** or discolored by gunpowder blasts. Tattooing ink was used to bring the color of their skin back to normal and make their injuries less noticeable.

## Cosmetic tattooing today

For a time, cosmetic tattooing went out of fashion. People became afraid of the idea of facial tattooing. After World War I, the cosmetics industry began to persuade women that it was acceptable for them to wear makeup rather than to have a "permanent beauty treatment." Today, however, cosmetic tattooing is making a comeback. It is used to outline eyebrows, or even replace them entirely if they have fallen out for some reason. Tattooing can even be used to make eyelashes look bigger and thicker, but the slightest mistake by the tattooist is disastrous. The tattooing is so close to the eye that it could easily be damaged, and the lid contains fine blood vessels that the tattooist has to be careful to avoid.

Cosmetic tattooing can also be used to reduce **smallpox** scars or **acne-pitting** of the skin, to make thin hair look thicker, or even to apply a permanent lipstick to a woman's lips. Facial tattooing is illegal in many countries, and usually only a licensed medical practitioner can apply cosmetic tattoos.

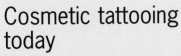

# Does It Hurt?

## Tattoos and pain

Getting a tattoo will almost certainly hurt to some extent. People have claimed otherwise. "Professor" George Burchett, one of the most famous tattooists, tattooed wealthy women, carnival performers, and even King Frederik of Denmark. Burchett claimed that "the normal tattooing operation is not painful—indeed, many of my clients have assured me that the 'prickle' is pleasant." Most people who have tattoos done admit it is, at best, uncomfortable, and can be extremely painful. Some people say that having a tattoo is like being snapped repeatedly with a rubber band. Others compare it to the feeling of an arm or leg being asleep.

**George Burchett (left) shows a client a tattoo that he designed for King Frederik of Denmark.**

The level of pain involved depends on where the tattoo is put on the body, the skill and training of the tattooist, and the customer's **pain threshold.** Fleshy parts of the body are far less painful than places where the skin is close to the bone, such as the ankle. Some tattooists, usually the most experienced, have a lighter touch than others. They are able to inject the ink at just the perfect depth to hit the **dermis** without going too deep and causing pain.

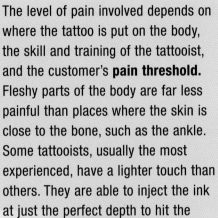

## Piercing and pain

The amount of pain involved in being pierced is hard to gauge because it depends on where the piercing is being done. Many people find that ear piercing is relatively painless, though afterwards the ears can throb for a while. Other piercings can be uncomfortable or even downright painful. Navel piercing, for example, goes through sensitive flesh and affects an area of the body that moves around a lot. Piercing the navel can be more painful than some other places, and the **wound** can be uncomfortable for a long time afterwards. It can take longer than a year for it to heal fully. The amount of pain also varies according to the skill of the piercer and how much pain the customer can withstand.

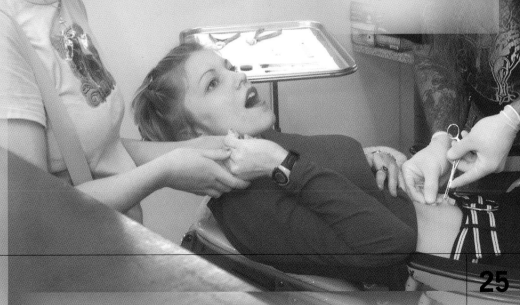

# Safe Tattoos and Piercings

There are health risks involved in having a tattoo done or being pierced. Tattoo and piercing parlors have to be very careful not to cause their customers harm. Reputable parlors, the ones that have a proper storefront and professional equipment, usually follow the safety rules. They also ask their customers health-related questions before starting work. **Backstreet** and traveling tattooists and body piercers may not be so careful. This means there is a greater risk of something going wrong. There are various signs that a tattoo or piercing parlor uses proper safety procedures.

## Disposables

To avoid the possibility of disease spreading from one person to the next, most pieces of equipment are used only once and then thrown away. Disposable tattoo equipment includes ink, ink cups, gloves, and tattoo needles. A good tattooist will show customers the new, unopened packages containing each of these before opening the seals on them in the customer's presence. The same is true of a professional piercer, who will break the seals on the needles in front of the customer. Piercing needles and the plastic tubes that surround them (which come in the same package) should be used only once, as should all antiseptic wipes and cloths.

**Autoclaves** such as this one are essential for keeping piercing and tattooing equipment as clean as possible.

## Autoclaves

Items that are reused in the tattooing or piercing processes need to be cleaned, then **sterilized** in an autoclave before they are used again. For tattooing, these include the needle bar and the tube; for piercing the only reusables are the clamps used to hold the flesh in position. Using an autoclave is the only way of killing microorganisms such as **viruses** or bacteria. Autoclaves work by heating the instruments to a very high temperature—sometimes as high as 270°F (132°C). Some items go through the autoclave in a special pouch. Once they have reached the correct temperature, an indicator strip on the pouch changes color.

# Pre-tattoo procedure

Good tattooists follow a careful procedure before starting a tattoo. They wash their hands, disinfect the work area, and put on a fresh pair of gloves. Next, the spray bottles that hold the ink are covered with plastic bags. Tattooists should then explain the **sterilization** procedure. After this, they will break the seals on the sterilized **autoclave** equipment and the single-use items, such as needles, in front of the customer. This ensures that everyone knows the correct equipment is being used. Once the skin has been washed and shaved to stop the needles from getting clogged with hair, and the transfer of the design has been applied, the tattooing can begin.

# Pre-piercing procedure

Piercing involves fewer pieces of equipment than tattooing, so the pre-piercing procedure is less complicated. If the area being pierced is hairy, the hair is shaved off. Then the clamps are taken out of the autoclave, and the work area is wiped clean with antiseptic, antibacterial wipes. Two dots are drawn on the skin to show where the piercing will enter and come out of the flesh. Once the customer is satisfied, the seal can be broken on the needle and the piercing can begin.

**A piercer wearing sterile gloves collects equipment together on a tray before beginning the piercing procedure.**

# Possible Problems

## Homemade tattoos

A study by the Children's Medical Center at the University of Massachusetts suggests that most teens get tattoos done by their friends, using pens, paper clips, and other unsuitable items. The risks involved in having this type of tattoo are relatively high. A tattoo done by a friend with little or no experience is unlikely to turn out as planned, which can lead to the loss of a friendship as well as an unwanted tattoo.

Homemade tattoos are also likely to be painful, because the tattooist will not know how far under the skin the ink has to be placed and may go too deep. There is a good chance that a homemade tattoo will become infected because the equipment used has not been properly **sterilized.**

**ffSoup for three weeks—it was all I could eat, my tongue was so swollen.JJ**

(Alex Johnson, 19, speaking about the effects of having a pierced tongue)

## Passing on blood-borne viruses

There are risks of passing on blood-borne **viruses,** both in tattooing and body piercing. The American Academy of Dermatology has recorded cases of blood-borne viruses, such as **hepatitis B,** being passed from one person to the next when equipment is not sterilized before being used. People carrying these viruses in their blood do not necessarily look ill and may not even be aware of the fact that they have a virus. Even if someone looks healthy they may not be, so using clean and safe equipment is always crucial.

## HIV and hepatitis C

There are no definite cases of **HIV** or **hepatitis C** being passed on through tattooing, although the risk does exist. Because the needles used are solid, not hollow like a syringe, passing on HIV or hepatitis C through tattooing is unlikely. In 2002, the Centers for Disease Control and Prevention determined that "no data exist in the United States indicating that persons with exposures

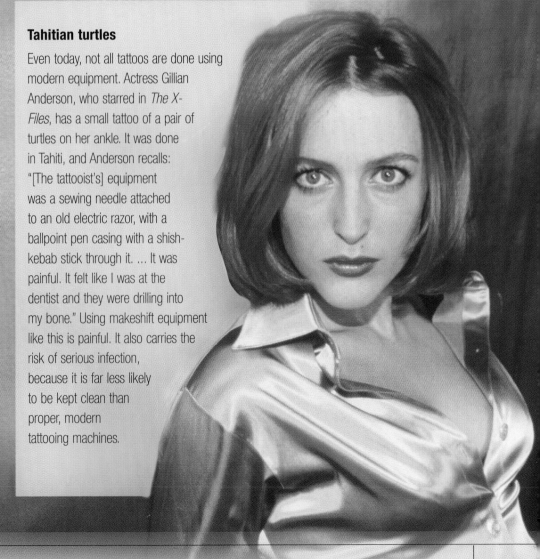

to tattooing and body piercing alone are at increased risk of hepatitis infection." The possibility of HIV or hepatitis C being passed on through piercing is theoretically far higher, because the needles used are hollow and offer a hiding place for the virus to survive. In a professional studio, only disposable needles should be used. **Backstreet** and traveling piercing studios are unlikely to have the same standards of **hygiene.**

### Tahitian turtles

Even today, not all tattoos are done using modern equipment. Actress Gillian Anderson, who starred in *The X-Files*, has a small tattoo of a pair of turtles on her ankle. It was done in Tahiti, and Anderson recalls: "[The tattooist's] equipment was a sewing needle attached to an old electric razor, with a ballpoint pen casing with a shish-kebab stick through it. ... It was painful. It felt like I was at the dentist and they were drilling into my bone." Using makeshift equipment like this is painful. It also carries the risk of serious infection, because it is far less likely to be kept clean than proper, modern tattooing machines.

## Post-procedure infections

In both tattooing and body piercing there is a risk of infection setting in after the tattoo or piercing is finished. This is why it is important to make sure everything is clean and **hygienic.** This is especially true in piercing. A navel piercing, for example, can take up to a year to fully heal. Unless a piercing is kept properly clean, the **wound** is likely to become infected. The surrounding flesh may swell up and the wound may start to seep fluid. If left unchecked, the flesh will start to grow against the jewelry, sealing it into the skin. At this point, the only way to remove the jewelry is to cut it out through minor **surgery.** Ear piercings can lead to an infection of the ear's cartilage, causing scarring.

## Allergic reactions

It is possible to have an **allergic reaction** to the ink that is used in tattooing. None of the 50 or so colors used in tattooing are **regulated** by the U.S. Food and Drug Administration, for example, so there are few guarantees that they have been fully tested as safe. The inks that were traditionally used in tattooing contained resins, acrylic, glycerol, or all three. But tattooists are now increasingly using **organic** pigments to help avoid allergic reactions.

# Piercing problems

Special problems can be caused if someone whose body is still growing has a piercing. The flesh surrounding a fourteen-year-old's navel, for example, is likely to change its shape over the next few years. If it is pierced, the hole made by the piercing is likely to change shape, too, possibly becoming uncomfortable and making it difficult to put jewelry inside.

Inexperienced piercers may pierce either too deep into the flesh or not deep enough. Eyebrow piercing, for example, is done at a depth of one-half inch (twelve millimeters). The healing process contracts the piercing slightly, bringing the depth to three-eighths inch (about ten millimeters). A piercing made at a lesser depth will contract to such a shallow depth that the surrounding skin will start to reject it and the piercing will grow out. Piercings that have been made too deep carry different problems. They bunch around the hole, making an ugly lump, and are uncomfortable and slow-healing as a result.

Other problems can also occur. The jewelry from tongue piercings can damage tooth enamel, painfully and sometimes **permanently.** Navel piercings can cause difficulties for women during pregnancy, as the skin around their stomach swells and the piercing becomes stretched out of shape.

# Caring for Tattoos and Piercings

Once a tattoo has been finished, it needs to be looked after carefully. There can be health problems if it has not healed properly, and the design can blur. All tattoos bleed slightly just after they are finished. This bleeding normally stops within a few minutes, but if the person being tattooed has been drinking alcohol or taking certain drugs, or has been tattooed over a scar, bleeding can continue.

## A healing tattoo

A new tattoo is bandaged in the tattoo parlor. The bandage needs to be removed about two hours later. The tattoo is then washed gently in mild antibacterial soap and patted dry. Rubbing dry a new tattoo can cause the colors and shape to blur. Then a very thin coat of ointment is gently worked into the skin. Too much ointment could pull the color out of the skin. Most tattooists warn that if it is possible to see the ointment on the skin, then too much is being used.

While a tattoo is healing, which usually takes anywhere between one and three weeks, it needs to be kept

New tattoos are often sore and inflamed just after being finished.

as dry as possible. Letting the shower pound down on it, soaking in a hot bath, and swimming in the sea or pools can all cause problems. Sometimes a scab forms on a tattoo that falls off on its own when the tattoo has healed. Any sign of infection must be treated by a doctor.

## Caring for a piercing

Caring for a new piercing mainly involves keeping it clean, especially until it has fully healed. The piercing has to be washed in the morning and evening with antibacterial soap. As soon as it is bearable, the jewelry keeping the **wound** open should be turned to prevent it from being sealed against the flesh. This routine needs to be followed until the piercing is completely healed, when all swelling and tenderness have disappeared. Once the wound has healed completely, it should still be cleaned regularly, using soap and possibly cotton swabs if the hole is large enough.

A new navel piercing is cleaned with a cotton swab and antibacterial liquid.

# Permanence

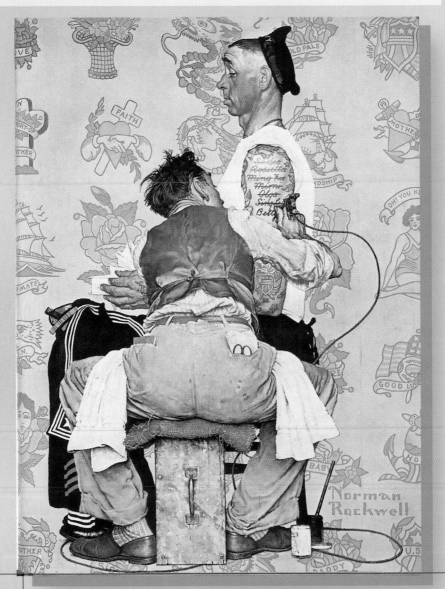

Tattoos are **permanent.** They are made by placing ink in a stable layer of skin that does not break down. Unless the ink is removed in some way, the tattoo remains forever. Until the late 1980s, the only way to remove a tattoo was to cut away the skin in which it was embedded. This was a painful procedure that left scarring.

The American Academy of Dermatology estimates that between 1979 and 2002, the number of registered tattoo parlors in the United States grew from 300 to more than 4,000. This growth has been matched in many other Western countries. As the number of people getting tattoos has grown, so has the number of people wanting to have their tattoos removed. A whole new technique that uses lasers to remove unwanted tattoos has recently been developed.

## Laser removal

Lasers remove tattoos by **vaporizing** the colors in the tattooing ink, using a high-intensity beam of light. One big problem with the laser removal of tattoos is the price. A medium-sized tattoo that costs about $75 to have made costs between $1,000 and $1,800 to remove.

## Permanent holes

Most piercings are also permanent. Once a piercing has healed, it will rarely completely close up. However, a piercing without jewelry in it is not as noticeable as a tattoo and is easier to forget or ignore.

**Left: A sailor has the name of yet another girlfriend crossed out when a new one is added!**

**Right: Holes left by piercings are usually inconspicuous unless they contain jewelry, but some holes can be enlarged to become very noticeable.**

# Impermanent Tattoos

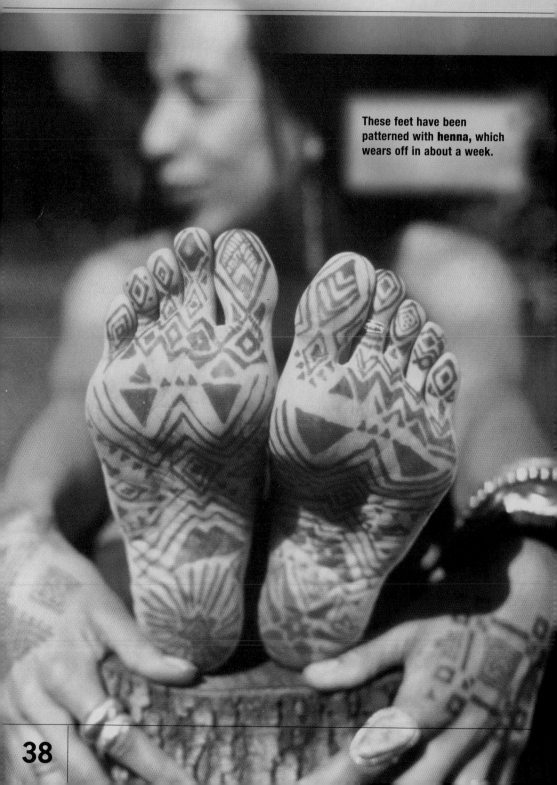

These feet have been patterned with **henna**, which wears off in about a week.

For people who are not 100-percent sure that they want a tattoo that will be with them for the rest of their life, there are less-than-**permanent** options. These include **temporary** tattoos that are stuck to the skin, henna tattoos that stain the outer layer of skin, and tattoos using ink that breaks down and disappears over a period of time.

## Temporary tattoos

Temporary tattoos are transfers that are added to the skin using water. The transfer is placed flat against the skin, then soaked in water. As the backing paper moistens it can be peeled away, leaving just the tattoo design on the skin. Temporary tattoos last up to seven days.

One of the advantages of temporary tattoos is that not only can you buy pre-designed transfers, but you can make up personal designs using kits available in some stores and over the Internet. People who are considering a permanent tattoo can design a temporary tattoo and wear it for up to seven days as a way of getting used to it. If the temporary tattoo no longer looks good to them after a week, they can decide not to have it done.

## Henna tattoos

Henna tattoos use a plant extract to stain the surface of the skin, usually with a dark brown color. These tattoos are temporary, and wear away as the surface of the skin is worn away and replaced with new skin. Henna designs are an ancient tradition, especially among people from India and the Middle East. Women there wear complicated designs on their hands and feet, often to mark special occasions. A woman who is about to get married may have very elaborate henna designs that take many hours to apply.

## Disappearing tattoos

Tattoos that last only a certain period of time before fading away and disappearing are now available. They are made in the same way as a permanent tattoo—by injecting ink or pigment into a lower layer of the skin—but the ink that is used breaks up and fades away in a period of three to five years.

# Making Decisions

Given the **permanence** of piercings and tattoos, people considering either should think very hard about what they are about to do. A tattoo of a cartoon character or the name of a rock band might be fashionable now, but will it just be an embarrassment at age 50? People who get a tattoo need to be very sure that it is what they want. They also need to be sure that the significance of the tattoo will stay with them for the rest of their life.

Piercing is in some ways less of a long-term issue than tattooing, because once the jewelry is removed, the piercing is less obvious. However, the social reactions to a visible piercing in an unusual place can be similar to tattoos. Some people want little or nothing to do with people who have obvious piercings. They may find piercings ugly, or not wish to be associated with someone who has marked himself or herself as different from most others. The scars are also visible for a long time, and a lot of facial piercings can dramatically affect a person's appearance.

Experts suggest that people follow certain guidelines to avoid being stuck with a tattoo or piercing they do not like or that causes problems later.

- People should never get tattooed or pierced while drunk or after taking drugs. Not only will they be unable to make clear decisions, but there are increased physical risks from prolonged bleeding.

- If possible, people should try out the tattoo or piercing before getting it done permanently. This is easier for a tattoo, as there are kits available that let people make a **temporary** version of the design they want. For piercing, people should spend some time imagining what effect the piercing will have. Would an eyebrow piercing catch on glasses, or a nose piercing create difficulties during a cold, for example?

- People should consider the possible effect of a tattoo or piercing on career prospects. Will it make a person less successful later on if he or she has the name of a rock band tattooed on the neck?

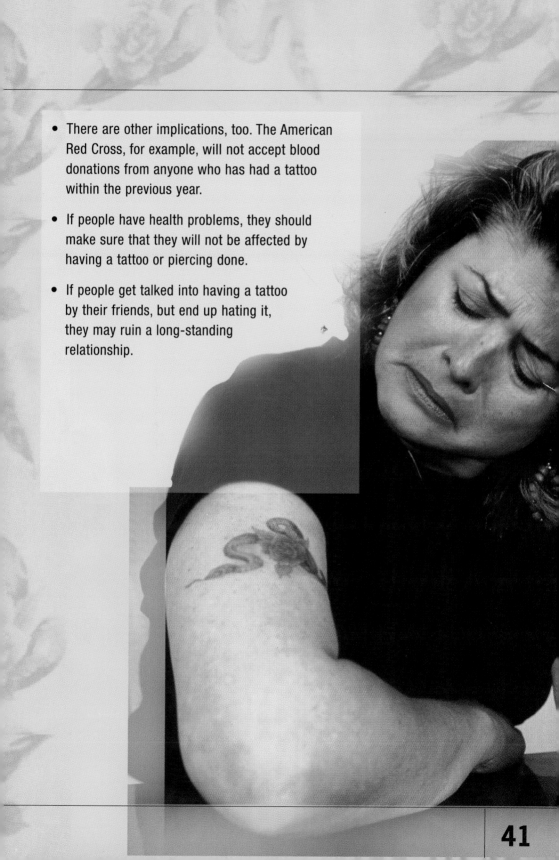

- There are other implications, too. The American Red Cross, for example, will not accept blood donations from anyone who has had a tattoo within the previous year.

- If people have health problems, they should make sure that they will not be affected by having a tattoo or piercing done.

- If people get talked into having a tattoo by their friends, but end up hating it, they may ruin a long-standing relationship.

# Positive Reactions

For many people, having a tattoo or a piercing is an uplifting experience. Usually, they have thought about why they want it done and have a special reason behind their decision. Once the tattoo or piercing is finished, it becomes part of them, something that has an important place in their life.

One woman interviewed for this book, Jinky James, has a tattoo hidden at the bottom of her back. It shows her family crest, the Sun with a face in the center. She had the tattoo done to remind her of her brother, who lives

### Memorial tattoos

On February 13, 1997, a professional surfer named Todd Chesser was killed in a big-wave surfing accident. Chesser was surfing with friends off the north shore of the Hawaiian island, Oahu. The waves were enormous: Chesser drowned when he was held underwater too long after falling from his surfboard. Chesser was one of the most popular surfers in Hawaii. His closest friends decided they would have tattoos done to remember him. Several of the world's best surfers now have tattoos with the words, "In Loving Memory of Todd Chesser."

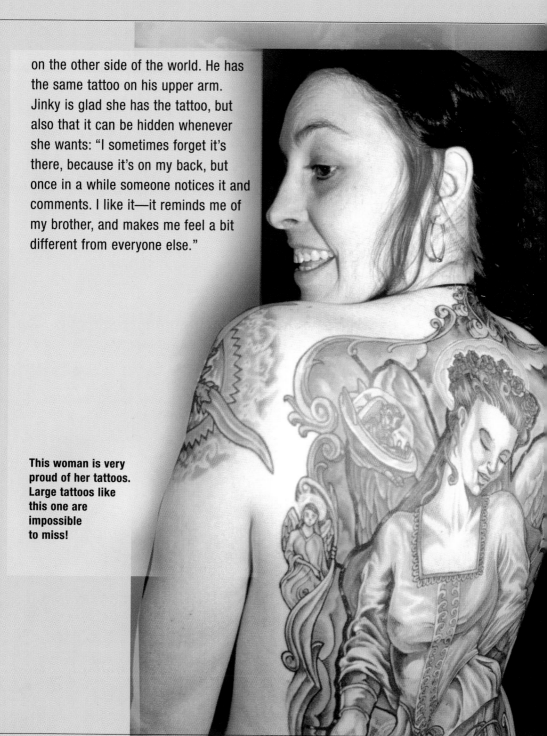

on the other side of the world. He has the same tattoo on his upper arm. Jinky is glad she has the tattoo, but also that it can be hidden whenever she wants: "I sometimes forget it's there, because it's on my back, but once in a while someone notices it and comments. I like it—it reminds me of my brother, and makes me feel a bit different from everyone else."

This woman is very proud of her tattoos. Large tattoos like this one are impossible to miss!

# Negative Reactions

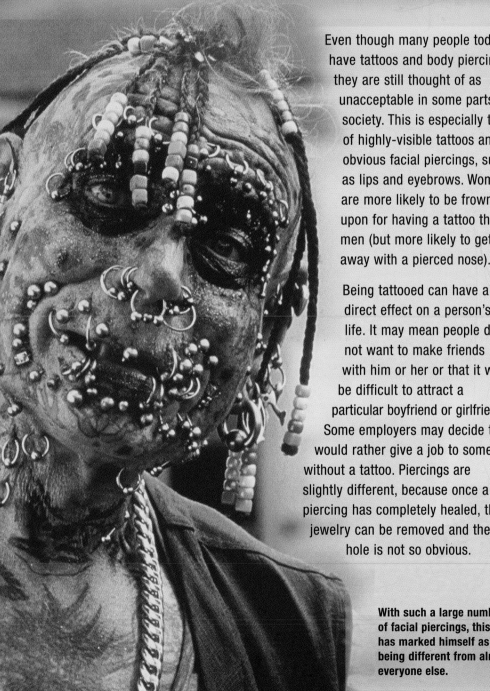

Even though many people today have tattoos and body piercings, they are still thought of as unacceptable in some parts of society. This is especially true of highly-visible tattoos and obvious facial piercings, such as lips and eyebrows. Women are more likely to be frowned upon for having a tattoo than men (but more likely to get away with a pierced nose).

Being tattooed can have a direct effect on a person's life. It may mean people do not want to make friends with him or her or that it will be difficult to attract a particular boyfriend or girlfriend. Some employers may decide they would rather give a job to someone without a tattoo. Piercings are slightly different, because once a piercing has completely healed, the jewelry can be removed and the hole is not so obvious.

**With such a large number of facial piercings, this man has marked himself as being different from almost everyone else.**

## Tattoo position

The position of a tattoo can be important. For example, a small design at the base of a person's spine is easily hidden. The person can wear practically any kinds of clothes, and the tattoo will remain hidden unless it is deliberately revealed. A large tattoo on someone's chest, arms, or legs (like the ones on the right) is harder to hide, especially in the summer. If the tattoo needs to be hidden, many types and styles of clothes suddenly become off-limits.

## Regrets

Some people who have had tattoos done may regret it later. There is a whole industry based around tattoo removal, and many tattooists are asked to adapt old tattoos to say or show something different. Most of the people who later regret their tattoos had them done when they were young, on impulse, while they were drunk, or by a friend.

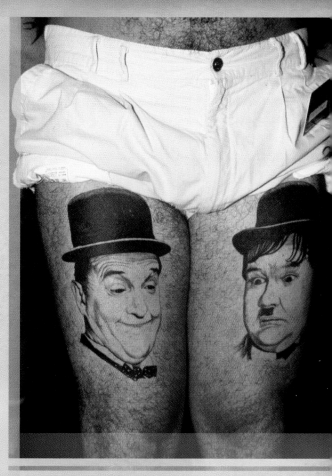

### Dexter Smith

Dexter Smith is a TV producer. He got a tattoo when he was 16 and, at the time, he was delighted with it. The tattoo is on his left shoulder and shows a small cartoon character. "It now looks stupid," says Dexter. "The colors have all run together because I was still growing when I had it done and they've stretched, and it looks like a blob. I wish I'd had it done later, I wish it was of something— anything!—other than what it's of, and most of all I wish I hadn't had it done at all."

# Getting Help

Tattoos and piercings can go wrong. They may become infected. Or a person might decide that he or she no longer wants a tattoo or piercing and needs advice about how to get rid of it.

## Immediate problems

When a tattoo or piercing becomes infected, it will develop some or all of the following signs:
- redness and soreness;
- swelling;
- high temperature;
- discharge of blood or pus oozing from the tattooed or pierced area;
- in the case of a piercing, the jewelry may become stuck and sealed into place.

If an infection develops, the only person who can provide proper help is a qualified medical professional.

## Later problems

If a person becomes worried that he or she may have contracted a disease such as **HIV, hepatitis B,** or **hepatitis C** through **unhygienic** conditions, for example, it is important to see a doctor as soon as possible. People who have developed a disease as a result of getting a tattoo or piercing will need further medical treatment. Their doctor will be able to send them to the appropriate **specialist** or **counselor** for further help. Customers are highly unlikely to catch a disease in a tattooing or piercing parlor that follows health procedures, according to the Centers for Disease Control and Prevention. **Backstreet** and traveling parlors, and tattoos and piercings that have been done by friends without the proper health procedures, offer a far higher possibility of infection. These places and people may not follow the same standards of **hygiene** and equipment as professional tattooists and piercers.

People who have decided that they no longer want their tattoo can discuss this with their doctor, who will be able to talk to them about the options. Usually the most realistic choice is simply to live with the tattoo, since the cost of having it removed is extremely high. However, people who have facial tattooing may be able to get help, either through counseling or removal.

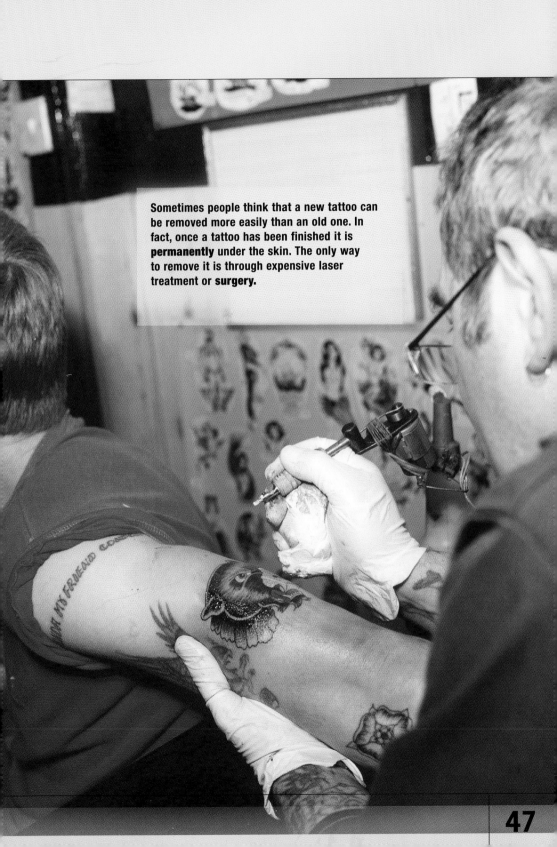

Sometimes people think that a new tattoo can be removed more easily than an old one. In fact, once a tattoo has been finished it is **permanently** under the skin. The only way to remove it is through expensive laser treatment or **surgery**.

## Treatment and removal

People with a piercing they no longer want can deal with it relatively easily. If they take out the jewelry inside the piercing, usually all that is visible will be a small hole at the entrance and exit of the piercing. This hole is likely to be **permanent,** and cannot be filled in except by tissue regrowing naturally in the hole. But in most cases the holes left by a piercing are usually hard to see, and easy to ignore if necessary.

A tattoo is harder to disguise than a piercing, especially if it has been done in an obvious place. Sometimes people feel they cannot live with their tattoo any longer. Until recently there would have been very little they could do except to have the skin in which the tattoo was embedded cut out, leaving a terrible scar. Today it is possible to have a tattoo removed using lasers.

People who decide that they no longer want a tattoo should first see their doctor, who will be able to give advice on where to get the tattoo removed as safely as possible.

## How tattoo removal works

Laser tattoo removal works by **vaporizing** the colors injected under the skin by the tattooist. Because certain colors only absorb some forms of light, different lasers have to be used to remove different colors. Black, which absorbs all forms of light, is the easiest tattoo color to remove; green and yellow are the most difficult. Removal of a complicated tattoo with lots of colors takes several visits.

Even though laser removal of a tattoo is less risky and painful than any other method, there are still risks. Most of these risks relate to what is left once the tattoo has been removed. Sometimes the skin either loses all its color or has too much color. Either way, a strange blotch is left behind. The site of the tattoo can also become infected, and there is a five percent chance that a permanent scar will be left behind.

Laser removal of a tattoo is an unrealistic option for most people because of the high cost. This means that nearly everyone who has a tattoo he or she no longer likes is stuck with it.

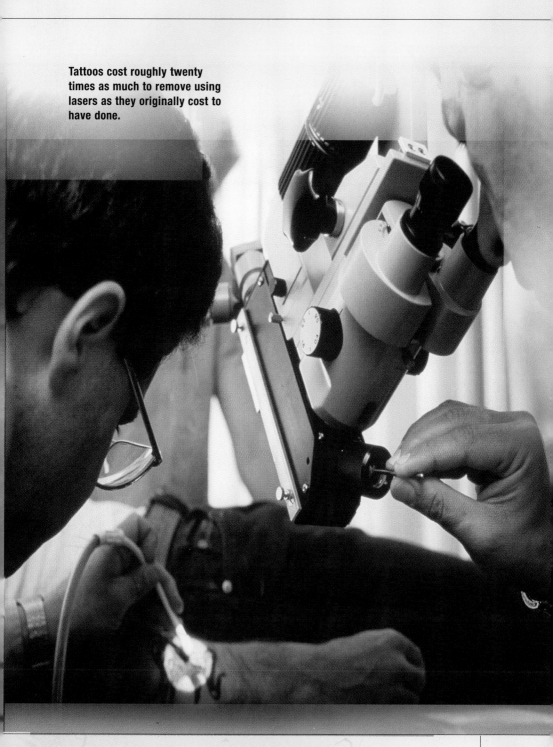

Tattoos cost roughly twenty times as much to remove using lasers as they originally cost to have done.

# Legal Matters

Most Western governments believe that young people under a certain age should not be allowed to have tattoos, and have made laws to stop them. Usually these laws say that young people should not be allowed to have a tattoo until they have become an adult, which is age eighteen in many countries. Stricter age limits have been encouraged by parents whose children have had tattoos done. For example, in Arizona the ban on tattooing for people under eighteen was linked to a campaign by a mother whose fifteen-year-old daughter came home with a tattoo.

Laws on age limits for having a piercing are less common, but piercing can be dealt with as an assault on a **minor.** If a minor gets a piercing without the permission of a parent or guardian, the police could become involved. If the parent makes a complaint, the piercer could be charged with assault or **wounding** and could end up in jail. Many piercing studios refuse to pierce people under the age of eighteen, partly because of the legal consequences and partly because there can be health problems with some piercings if they are done at a young age.

## Health regulation

Regulations covering health and safety requirements vary from one country to another, and even within a country. In 2002, nearly every U.S. state had some sort of regulations or age minimums for tattooing and tattoo parlors, but these vary greatly from state to state.

In Europe, Australia, and New Zealand, regulations tend to be tougher. Licensed tattoo and piercing parlors need to satisfy strict requirements. Studios that do not meet the requirements are not licensed and unable to stay in business for long.

# Showing identification

Any reputable tattoo or piercing parlor will insist on seeing identification (ID) before accepting a young client. They will normally only accept a photo ID to make sure that the customer is really the owner of the ID.

### Tattooing and the law

In many countries, tattooing tends to be governed by state law rather than federal law, so regulations will vary from one part of the country to another. In the United Kingdom, the Tattooing of Minors Act 1969 makes it illegal to tattoo anyone under the age of eighteen.

# Information and Advice

People who have a problem as a result of tattooing or body piercing should contact their doctor. Usually it is best to get advice as quickly as possible. A doctor may be able to provide pamphlets for patients to take and read, and will normally be able to find out where patients can go for counseling or tattoo-removal advice.

Information about tattooing and body piercing is fairly limited. Readers tempted to find out more about these subjects may be able to find some information from local libraries. There are also lots of books showing photos of tattoos and body piercings.

One of the best places for information about tattooing is the Internet. Information on body piercing is also available on the Internet, but it is harder to find informative or useful websites.

## Contacts

**Alliance of Professional Tattooists**
**2108 S. Alveron Way**
**Tucson, AZ 85711**
**(520) 514-5549**
*http://www.safe-tattoos.com*

This is a nonprofit organization that addresses the health and safety issues facing the tattoo industry.

**Association of Professional Piercers**
**PMB 286**
**5456 Peachtree Industrial Blvd.**
**Chamblee, GA 30341**
**(972) 720-0APP; (888) 888-1APP**
*http://www.safepiercing.org*

The APP is an international nonprofit organization dedicated to providing vital health and safety information relating to body piercing to piercers, health care providers, and the general public.

**Tattoo Archive**
**2804 San Pablo Avenue**
**Berkeley, CA 94702**
**(510) 548-5895**
*http://www.tattooarchive.com*

This website has information on subjects such as The Great Omi. The site also contains a variety of articles about the historical and cultural significance of tattooing, including information on the Maori of New Zealand.

# More Books to Read

Aronson, Virginia. *Everything You Need to Know about Hepatitis*. New York: Rosen Publishing Group, Inc., 2000.

Hayhurst, Chris. *Everything You Need to Know about Hepatitis C.* New York: Rosen Publishing Group, Inc., 2002.

Reybold, Laura. *Everything You Need to Know about the Dangers of Tattooing and Body Piercing.* New York: Rosen Publishing Group, Inc., 2000.

Weiss, Stefanie Iris. *Everything You Need to Know about Mehndi, Temporary Tattoos, and Other Body Arts.* New York: Rosen Publishing Group, Inc., 2000.

Winkler, Kathleen. *Tattooing and Body Piercing: Understanding the Risks.* Berkeley Heights, N.J.: Enslow Publishers, Inc., 2002.

# Glossary

**acne pitting**  minor scars caused by the skin condition acne

**allergy**  unexpected and unpleasant physical reaction to something. The reaction is known as an *allergic reaction.*

**antisocial**  behavior that goes against socially accepted ways of behaving

**autoclave**  high-temperature device that kills any germs inside it. Autoclaves are used by tattooists and piercers to sterilize their reusable equipment.

**backstreet**  term used to describe something that is hidden, secretive, and often illegal

**chisel**  bar of metal or wood with one flat end and one sharp end; the flat end is hit with a hammer to drive the sharp end into or under something

**counselor**  professional person who listens to someone talk through a problem, without being judgmental

**dermis**  inner layer of a human's skin

**freak show**  popular form of entertainment during the 19th century. Freak shows contained all sorts of unusual things, such as oddly-tattooed people or bearded women. These shows are considered cruel today since they profit from people's misfortunes.

**glacier**  thick sheet of ice that flows out of a snow-bound valley

**gladiator**  Roman slave who was paid to fight dangerous animals or fierce warriors to entertain crowds of people

**Hell's Angel**  member of a specific gang of motorcyclists famous for their lawless behavior

**henna**  reddish brown dye obtained from leaves of the henna plant

**hepatitis B**  virus that can be passed from one person to another by infected blood and blood products. The infection can sometimes be fatal.

**hepatitis C**  virus that can be passed from one person to another by infected blood, blood products, or shared drug needles. The infection can cause long-term liver damage

**HIV**  Human Immunodeficiency Virus. HIV attacks and destroys the body's immune system.

**hygiene**  cleanliness and healthiness. Something that is clean and germ-free is *hygienic.*

**lubricant**  agent, such as a gel or a cream, that is used to reduce friction between two objects that rub together

**Maori**  first humans to live in New Zealand, and their descendants

**minor**  person who has not reached full legal age

**mummified**  preserved after death through drying out

**Olympic rings**  five inter-linked rings that make up the symbol of the Olympic Games

**organic** grown without the use of artificial fertilizers or other chemicals

**pain threshold** level of pain a person can withstand

**permanent** not removable

**piercing gun** mechanical device that is sometimes used to perform piercings. Most professional piercers say that hand-held needles are more hygienic than piercing guns, because they are thrown away after a single use and thus cannot pass on diseases to other people.

**Polynesian** term used to describe something or someone that comes from Polynesia—an area in the Pacific Ocean

**regulate** to govern by a set of rules and regulations, usually those made and enforced by the government or the state

**Roman legion** name for a unit into which the armies of ancient Rome were organized

**shrapnel** pieces of metal created when a bomb or shell explodes. The bomb or shell case breaks apart; the pieces are known as shrapnel.

**smallpox** highly infectious disease that killed many people until the 20th century. Those who survived smallpox were often left with scarring on their face and elsewhere.

**specialist** someone who is an expert in a particular subject in the medical world

**stencil** outline of a shape that can either be filled in to make a finished picture or left as an outline

**sterilize** to clean, so that any germs or viruses are killed and cannot spread further infection. Equipment that is used in the piercing or tattooing process must be sterile.

**surgery** medical procedure that involves a doctor or surgeon cutting the skin of a patient

**symbolic** when one thing stands for another. For example, a country's flag can be a symbol for the nation.

**temporary** not permanent

**unhygienic** not clean

**vaporize** to turn into vapor; to change from solid or liquid form into a gas

**virus** microorganism or molecule that causes an infectious disease

**wound** cut or hole in flesh

# Index